Classic Convertibles

Classic
Convertibles

Over 35 timeless open-top designs

Chris Rees

LORENZ BOOKS

First published in 1999 by Lorenz Books

Lorenz Books is an imprint of
Anness Publishing Limited
Hermes House
88–89 Blackfriars Road
London SE1 8HA

© Anness Publishing Limited 1999

Published in the USA by Lorenz Books,
Anness Publishing Inc., 27 West 20th Street, New York,
NY 10011; (800) 354 9657

A CIP catalogue for this book is available from the British Library.

ISBN 1 85967 889 0

Publisher: **Joanna Lorenz**
Project Editor: **Zoe Antoniou**
Designer: **Simon Wilder**
Production Controller: **Joanna King**
Editorial Reader: **Joy Wotton**

Printed and bound in Singapore

10 9 8 7 6 5 4 3 2 1

CONTENTS

When the clouds part and summer is allowed its full rein, owners of ordinary cars turn green with envy. For on the roads, those who have weathered the winter in their convertibles can finally justify their choice. Driving top down with the wind in your hair just feels so right. On a hot summer's day it is the only way to travel.

INTRODUCTION

In the early days of motoring, all cars were open-topped. More often than not, the vehicles had no roof at all because the engineers who built these pioneers were more interested in the technical hurdles than comfort or aesthetics. When the market for cars first began to emerge, it was inevitably dominated by the wealthy, and this group soon demanded the sort of protection from the elements that was afforded by their horse and carriage. As a result, the optional roof was developed and the first exclusive convertibles appeared.

It was during the 1920s that convertibles became a very popular means of transport. As their number increased, it became cheaper to buy open tourers than fully enclosed coachbuilt bodies that had become available and which had now entered the luxury end of the market. Cars, such as the Ford Model T and Austin Seven were particularly "popular" models.

After World War II, the market changed again. The convertible began to decline in importance altogether as closed saloon cars, with their more practical appeal, came down in price. Convertible models began to assume a more glamorous image once again and the open-top became a dominant feature of sports cars for the first time, an association which remains today.

In the 1950s, the market for convertibles was still fairly exclusive but stable. Most car manufacturers offered at least one drop-top model in their range. By the 1960s, however, the idea of open-top versions

Above: **The open "tourer" style was the way in which most cars were delivered in the early years. This Austin Seven was one of the cheapest cars available in the 1920s, and its folding roof was a contributing factor, helping to keep cars inexpensive and, as a result, popular.**

Left: **Excellent coachwork was made by some specialist companies during the 1930s, on chassis that were supplied by prestige car makers, such as the Delahaye. It was during this period that convertibles were perhaps at their most opulent and elegant.**

Right: **For almost sixty years, the Ford Model T remained the world s most popular car. Its success was founded on solid engineering at very cheap prices. Indeed, the open-topped model was the most inexpensive way to produce a car at that time.**

Below: **Delage was one of the most prestigious manufacturers in the world, and some of the most respected coachbuilders created spectacular drophead coachwork on Delage chassis. These included dream-like bodies Labourdette, Chapron and Saoutchik.**

of ordinary saloons greatly declined in importance, and by the 1970s had almost died out completely due to the fear that American Federal law would ban open cars on safety grounds, although this did not actually happen.

During the 1980s, a whole new dawn began for the convertible and today the market remains strong. Whether it is enjoyed as an exclusive object, or even just for fun, the open-top is once again something to be desired.

With such a vast number of convertibles to choose from this collection can in no way be seen as a definitive guide. However, it will certainly provide an invaluable and exciting introduction to some of the most classic convertible cars from around the world. There is much to celebrate here, whatever your personal favourite, to suit the tastes of every car enthusiast .

Right: **In the post-war years, the convertible saloon still occupied an important position in the marketplace. Cars such as the Sunbeam Rapier offered a stylish and yet inexpensive way to travel four-up.**

8

SOFT TOPS

The word "convertible" or "cabriolet" encompasses a multitude of varied open-topped forms. As many different technologies and different fashions have evolved, the soft top has developed in a variety of ways. In some cases, a roof may be partly or even completely removed, or it may fold neatly down and out of the way. Driving *al fresco* can encompass an exciting variety of options and experiences.

Porsche, for example, offered its first convertible in 1951 with the traditional folding soft roof, which is unhitched from the screen rail and folded up behind the seats. Then in 1954, Porsche developed the Speedster, with a cut-down windscreen (windshield) and very low soft top.

For the 911 of 1965, Porsche abandoned the idea of full convertibles and instead adopted an idea that was pioneered by Triumph in the TR4. The new system incorporated a fixed steel roll-over bar and a lift-out roof panel that could be stored in the boot (trunk). This design retained many of the virtues of a coupé (rigidity, safety and weather sealing) but kept some of the open-top experience. Porsche called its car the Targa, a name that has stuck more than Triumph's description of it as a Surrey top. In the early days, the 911's curved rear screen could be removed, but it became fixed soon after.

Above: **Ferrari has always offered convertibles in its model range but rarely as the only choice for its fastest and most expensive model. The F50 was offered in open form. Of course, most owners would only be taking their car out in fine weather, but if rain looked likely, you could fit a special hard top supplied. The problem was, if you left it at home and got caught in a shower, there was no alternative but to get wet.**

Above: **Lamborghini's dramatic Diablo Roadster cleverly incorporated a solid roof panel that could be removed and placed over the mid-mounted engine when the sun began to shine.**

Above: **Here is a novel variation on the open roof theme. Porsche's 1989 Panamericana prototype featured a completely removable roof and rear window for the best of both worlds – coupé and convertible.**

Porsche returned to the full cabriolet style in the 1980s and also proposed a concept car called the Panamericana. This had a totally removable roof and rear window but never made production.

Another popular way to open up to the elements was the roll-top roof, which was basically a sunroof that folded right back to the base of the rear window. This typically featured on cheap cars such as the Fiat Topolino and Autobianchi Bianchina and was developed partly for fun and partly for practicality. The idea made a comeback in Nissan's quirky "retro" Figaro in 1990.

In the old days, sports cars had fully removable soft tops that merely attached to the body via pop fasteners. These days, some exotic cars also have removable roofs

but these are hard tops. In the case of the Lamborghini Diablo Roadster, the roof can be fixed over the engine cover and put back on if the weather changes. As for the Ferrari F50, you have to leave the hard top behind in the garage and hope that it doesn't rain.

Other styles include the Landaulette (a limousine with a fold-down rear section),

Above: **Porsche did not invent the "targa" top, but it made the idea very much its own. Stiffness was kept in the bodyshell by retaining a fixed roll-over bar, while the roof panel could be lifted out and stored in the trunk (boot).**

Left: **Soft tops are often criticized for being flappy, leaky and draughty, yet everyone knows a sports car should have an open roof. Suzuki's solution to this conundrum was to install a folding hard top for its little Cappuccino. The rigid rear section simply folded away out of sight.**

the Sedanca de Ville (where the front part of the roof is open) and more unique set-ups, such as the one used for the Suzuki Cappuccino where the roof is made up of a combination of elements: in this case, separate solid targa roof panels, a T-bar in the centre and a solid rear section that disappears down into the body.

ALFA ROMEO SPIDER

The word "Spider" really belongs to Alfa Romeo, and through successive generations it has been the Italian company's badge for its charismatic sports cars. Spider, as used here, has nothing to do with hair and multiple legs. The word comes from the last century, and was used to describe a light two-wheeled carriage.

The classic incarnation of the Spider ran from 1966 to 1994. Ironically, it began life as the Duetto, a name chosen through a competition, but everyone called it Spider anyway, and within two years Alfa Romeo had officially renamed it Spider.

This was a true sports car in every sense. Its handsome bodywork was styled by Pininfarina, which was, amazingly, viewed as quite controversial in its day, while its mechanical side derived from the Giulia series. This meant sweet twin-cam all-alloy

engines, disc brakes on all four wheels, fine suspension and a five-speed gearbox. That was sophisticated stuff for 1966, and the Spider was extremely rewarding to drive.

The Spider grew up over the years, its engine enlarging from 1600cc to 1750cc and finally to 2000cc. The original "cuttle-fish" tail was chopped off in 1970 to create a more aerodynamic shape. The model lasted until 1994, latterly with a very smart Pininfarina redesign, before being replaced by a new Spider. This was a dramatically styled car featuring twin headlights behind a clamshell bonnet (hood), and a rising body feature line with a sporting interior.

Below: **The Spider was a true sports car, mostly recognized as a classic in the years from 1966 to 1994.**

Above: **The Spider's cabin was an object lesson in sports car simplicity with its plain yet supportive seating, practical rubber matting and a wood-rim steering wheel. It was certainly a sophisticated interior.**

ALFA ROMEO SPIDER 1966–94

⚙ **BODY/CHASSIS** Integral chassis with two-door body in steel.

⚙ **ENGINE** Aluminium four-cylinder twin cam, from 1290cc to 1962cc, 87 bhp to 131 bhp.

⚙ **TRANSMISSION** Five-speed manual, rear-wheel drive.

⚙ **SUSPENSION** Front: unequal-length control arms, coil springs. Rear: rigid axle with trailing links, upper arms and coil springs.

Above: **Two decades separate these Alfa Romeo Spiders, yet they were basically the same design. The early "round-tail" car in the foreground has a purity of line lost in later examples. The car towards the rear is a "Series 3" Aerodynamic model with black plastic spoilers.**

Left: **Any Alfa Romeo consists of an engine first and foremost and everything else comes "for free". The Spider was always fitted with an advanced, sweet twin-cam all-alloy four-cylinder engine. In Europe this was a twin carburettor unit for most of the model's life. In America fuel injection was fitted from 1969 onwards.**

ASTON MARTIN DB6 VOLANTE

Prince Charles still drives one, and that just about sums up the strong aristocratic charms of this essentially British sports car. Indeed, Aston Martin is itself part of a rich tradition of classic and elite cars and its convertibles play a prominent role in the company's history. The "DB" line began in 1947, the letters refering to Sir David Brown who owned Aston Martin from 1947 to 1972. The DB6 arrived in 1965 and since then, Aston Martin have always referred to their convertibles by the name Volante.

The DB6 was the last of the classic six-cylinder DB Astons, and it is widely regarded as the most handsome of them all. It had a longer wheelbase than the earlier DB5 (the one that James Bond famously drove) and a cut-off tail with a kicked-up rear spoiler.

This was an extremely luxurious machine, boasting a generous array of instruments, including electric windows, air conditioning, a power aerial (antenna), leather upholstery and a power-operated folding roof that stowed neatly away.

The 4 litre engine developed 282 bhp or, in the finely tuned Vantage engine, no less than 325 bhp. This was enough for a top speed of 155mph (240kph). For a continental dash to St Tropez, there was not a more capable car than this. It may well have been

Above: **The fabulous all-alloy 4 litre six-cylinder engine gave the DB6 a tremendous turn of speed, especially in Vantage tune, when a top speed of around 155mph (240kph) was quoted. It was one of the world's most expensive cars in its day, and it is still one of the ultimate grand tourers.**

Above: **Classic British elegance emanated from the DB6's cabin. Fine quality carpet, leather upholstery and a very generous array of instruments distinguished this elegant and sporting cockpit. The Aston Martin became the epitome of British style particularly through the association of earlier models with James Bond films.**

one of the world's most expensive cars in its day, but this was in many ways the ultimate thoroughbred grand tourer. When the DB6 left production in 1970, there was no direct convertible replacement. Indeed, the next drop-top Aston was eight years off and, of course, it could only have one name and that was Volante.

The new DB7 Volante made quite an immediate impact in sales terms. It boosted Aston Martin's production levels to an unprecedented high, especially in America. Ford became the new owner of Aston Martin in 1987 and a new model programme soon began, which has proved to be very popular and successful.

Below: **No car sums up the qualities of this very British convertible craft more completely than the Aston Martin DB6 Volante. It was exquisitely well built and beautifully designed. With sound engineering and a capacity for being extremely fast, it was an astounding car. The DB7 immediately made an impact in sales terms, but the DB6 still remains the most handsome classic.**

ASTON MARTIN DB6 VOLANTE 1965–70

⚝ **BODY/CHASSIS** Unitary platform chassis with two-door body in aluminium.

⚝ **ENGINE** Alloy in-line six-cylinder twin cam, 3995cc, 282 bhp to 325 bhp.

⚝ **TRANSMISSION** Five-speed manual or Borg-Warner three-speed automatic, rear-wheel drive.

⚝ **SUSPENSION** Front: upper/lower control arms, coil springs. Rear: rigid axle with Watts linkage, radius rods and coil springs.

AUSTIN-HEALEY 3000

onald Healey's brilliant sports car was snapped up by Austin as soon as its chairman, Leonard Lord, first set eyes on it at the 1953 London Motor Show. A new marque, Austin-Healey, was then formed to produce the handsome new sports machine and it certainly took the world by storm. This Healey 100 had a 2.6 litre four-cylinder engine from the Austin Atlantic, and bodies were built by Jensen, central England, with final assembly at the MG factory.

In its ultimate guise from 1959, it was renamed the 3000 to celebrate the fact that its six-cylinder engine had now grown to 3 litres. It has since become known as the "Big Healey", a fitting title for the fastest member of the family. You could expect a top speed approaching 120mph (192kph)

Right: **The cabin of the 3000 MkIII reflects classic British sports car themes, descended from the 1950s. The seats are upholstered in leather, the doors and console are trimmed in matching colour, the wood-rim alloy-spoked steering wheel has never been bettered, the facia has elegant walnut veneer and the instruments are grouped directly in front of the driver for readability.**

Below: **Sublimely beautiful on the outside, yet rugged and powerful under the skin, the Austin-Healey 3000 offered an impressively complete sports car package at a price that embarrassed other, lesser, sports cars, and its performance levels were extremely high.**

AUSTIN-HEALEY 3000 1959–68

⊕ **BODY/CHASSIS** Separate ladder chassis with two-door body in steel.

⊕ **ENGINE** Cast-iron in-line six-cylinder overhead valve, 2912cc, 124 bhp to 148 bhp.

⊕ **TRANSMISSION** Four-speed manual with optional overdrive, rear-wheel drive.

⊕ **SUSPENSION** Front: wishbones with coil springs. Rear: rigid axle with semi-elliptic leaf springs.

Right: **There was something in the Big Healey's clean shape that held the very essence of a sports car. It offered "big bang" performance and feel, yet was priced very reasonably. It duly decimated the ranks of specialist sports car makers in Britain. This is a 1961 MkI.**

for most versions and new front disk brakes that improved its stopping power.

This was a big, brawny, old school sports car. You needed muscles to manhandle the steering and depress the clutch, and to start with there were no winding windows, just detachable curtains. The 3000 could be ordered as a two-seater or as a 2+2 with a small space for children in the back.

The Healey's demise in 1968 had more to do with American safety laws than any drop in demand. North America was always the car's biggest market, and its production suffered badly. The British Leyland Motor Corporation tried to replace it with a six-cylinder MG called the MGC, but it was a scant substitute for the old Healey and it was ultimately far less successful.

Left: **Despite its origins in a pre-war truck, the Healey's in-line six-cylinder engine was highly effective in this sports car setting. In its ultimate 3 litre guise it could develop 148 bhp, enough for a top speed of 121mph (194kph) and a 0–60mph (0–96kph) time of 9.8 seconds. This was a brawny machine in all respects.**

Below: **The winged Austin-Healey badge symbolized the effective merger of Donald Healey's sports car expertise with giant Austin's production and distribution network.**

17

CADILLAC ELDORADO

There is no greater icon of the golden era of fins 'n' chrome than the 1959 Cadillac Eldorado. This was the year that everyone tried to out-do everyone else with bigger fins and more ornate chrome-work, and Cadillac won. Its cliff-sized rear fins, rocket-ship rear light clusters and fridge-sized chrome bumpers were the most extreme expression of that glitzy era of excess. The '59 Cadillacs were available in a variety of body styles, but only one really matters to collectors these days and that is the Eldorado Biarritz convertible. In its day it was the cream of American cars, costing $7401 (£4900), over $2500 (£1670) more than the entry-level '59 Caddy coupé.

Underneath the mechanical side was very familiar, but for the '59 the V8 engine was even bigger (up to 6384cc), the power output rose (to 345 bhp on the Eldorado) and both the power steering and suspension were greatly improved.

This car had everything. A power top was essential, of course, and the interior reeked of chrome-laden rock-and-roll influence, brimming with bright colours and a sparkling jukebox style. Painted pink, the Eldorado became an essential extra in innumerable Hollywood movies. Its styling may have been overblown and gimmicky, but it is still the case that Harley Earl's '59 Caddy will be remembered forever as the epitome of 1950s Americana.

Right: **Virtually no other American car can hold a candle to the legendary status of the 1959 Cadillac Eldorado Biarritz convertible. In terms of size, presence and sheer extravagance, Harley Earl's crowning glory of the fins 'n' chrome era remains an icon of 1950s America.**

CADILLAC ELDORADO 1959

⊛ **BODY/CHASSIS** Separate ladder chassis with two-door body in steel.

⊛ **ENGINE** Cast-iron V8-cylinder overhead valve, 6384cc, 345 bhp.

⊛ **TRANSMISSION** Three-speed automatic, rear-wheel drive.

⊛ **SUSPENSION** Front: independent with coil springs. Rear: rigid axle with coil springs.

Below: **It was thanks to Harley Earl that Cadillac invented fins. Through the 1950s, they grew progressively larger and were taken to extremes in the 1958 model, shown below, which exhibited a rocket ship influence. However, it still was not quite as phantasmagorical as the '59 was to be and which is remembered as the truly classic car.**

CHEVROLET CORVETTE

For decades the aspirations of the American public towards sports cars have been directed at one home-grown product, the Chevrolet Corvette. As America's only real sports car, it has had to carry a lot of expectation, but it has always won through.

The line began in 1953 with the world's first-ever mass-produced glassfibre (fiber-glass) car. Ever since the 'Vette has had a plastic body. In those early days, the body style was open sports only and there was no coupé style. A second series arrived in

1955 with scalloped sides and tuned V8 engines, which provided a performance that was on a higher plane.

The classic Sting Ray appeared in 1963, with shark-like styling from the pen of Bill Mitchell. It featured a boat-tail rear end, humped wings and a huge 7 litre V8 option with up to 435 bhp on tap. A portent of things to come, there was now a coupé body style as well. The new Sting Ray arrived in 1967, and similarly, it was also

Above: **The Mako Shark was a "dream car" styling exercise done by Bill Mitchell on the Corvette. Echoing a shark-like profile, with inlets for gills and exhaust pipes for fins, it directly inspired the production of the Corvette Sting Ray of 1963.**

Right: **The original Corvette was quite a strange beast — a plastic-bodied, stripped-out sports car that America had a hard time taking to its heart. That has all changed today, as it has become very sought-after. This is an early example from 1953.**

Right: **The classic Sting Ray Corvette of the 1960s merged shark-like lines with muscle car power.**

Left: **The 'Vette was brought bang up to date in 1983 with a new shape that lent itself superbly to the drop-top style.**

Right: **Bold colours, aero-style dials and a red-rim steering wheel have now all come to symbolize pure Americana.**

Below left: **The classic Corvette emblem, showing two crossed flags.**

CHEVROLET CORVETTE 1998

⊕ **BODY/CHASSIS** Steel chassis frame with two-door body in plastic.

⊕ **ENGINE** Aluminium V8-cylinder overhead cam, 5665cc, 345 bhp.

⊕ **TRANSMISSION** Six-speed manual or four-speed automatic, rear-wheel drive.

⊕ **SUSPENSION** Front: double wishbones with coil springs. Rear: double wishbones with coil springs.

sold in both convertible and coupé forms, the latter a targa style with removable roof panels. By 1975, however, the convertible had been dropped from the price lists.

It took until ten years later for Chevrolet to come up with another drop-top 'Vette. This was the handsome all-new Corvette for the 1980s. Some body strengthening was required, but it looked very clean and was an excellent performer.

The Corvette entered its latest generation in 1997 and again there was a convertible version. With a 0–60mph (0–96kph) time of 5.0 seconds and a top speed of 171mph (275kph), this model was a genuine world-class supercar.

21

CHEVROLET 1955-57

The so-called Tri-Chevys are the range of models that Chevrolet made in the three years from 1955 to 1957. These have now become the very essence of the Golden Era of American style in the 1950s. Not only was the Chevy one of America's best-selling cars ever, it was also one of the most exciting. The Bel Air was the most glamorous of the designs, and as a convertible it was also the most expensive. It is small wonder that today it is one of the great American classics.

In styling terms, it has stood the test of time, stopping short of the excesses of the fins 'n' chrome era and looking sharp and relatively clean. The Bel Air and the rest of the Chevy family incorporated that very fashionable '50s feature, panoramic windscreens (windshields). The fad arrived with the '55 models and became a standard Detroit feature for many years.

The Chevy was powered by a true milestone engine, able to rev freely, weighing less than GM's old six-cylinder engine and yet being very powerful. For the '57, it developed 185 bhp in standard form, but there were four optional stages if you wanted more power, from a mild 220 bhp tune right up to a 283 bhp version whose power came courtesy of Ramjet fuel injection at an extra cost of $500 (£340). This enabled Chevrolet to claim one horsepower per

Below: **With bullet-like chrome around the front end, the 1957 Bel Air was one of the best-loved cars of all time in America.**

CHEVROLET BEL AIR CONVERTIBLE

⚙ **BODY/CHASSIS** Separate steel chassis with two-door body in steel.

⚙ **ENGINE** Cast-iron V8-cylinder overhead valve, 4342cc/4637cc, 162–283 bhp.

⚙ **TRANSMISSION** Two-speed automatic, rear-wheel drive.

⚙ **SUSPENSION** Front: wishbones with coil springs. Rear: rigid axle with leaf springs.

cubic inch, making it the first production engine ever to do so, apart from the Chrysler's '56 300B. In addition to this, the Chevy was also a cut above other cars for driving, and in 1955 *Motor Trend* magazine voted it "Best Handling" car for that year. Indeed, history recalls the Tri-Chevy as one of the great defining moments in American culture, and even perhaps the pinnacle of the popular style decade.

Above: **The top folded neatly away below decks, allowing the passengers to enjoy the experience of travelling fast in style.**

Right: **The '57 Chevy Bel Air is rightly regarded as probably the most pivotal American car design of the 1950s, combining sound engineering with clean good looks that stopped short of the fins 'n' chrome excesses.**

NEO-CLASSICS

Given that the golden age of the automobile was the ten years preceding the Second World War, it is not surprising that many people still yearn for the fabulous machines that seemed so out-of-reach at the time. Modern technology makes duplicating the style of these extravagant classics both relatively simple and reliable, and has given rise to the neo-classic, which is a vintage car on the outside and a modern car underneath.

The first company to bring the 1930s to the modern age was an American company called Excalibur, which was run by Brooks Stevens. Stevens first had the idea of recreating old classics as early as 1951 in a small

Right and below: **The notion of cars as "classics" did not really arrive until the 1960s, and Brooks Stevens paid tribute to one of the greatest of them all, the Mercedes-Benz SSK, with his Excalibur SS, first seen in 1964. Its extrovert character and high prices made it a favourite of Hollywood film stars, but it was also a very fast and exciting sports car.**

series of "modern vintage" racers. His real passion, however, was the Mercedes-Benz SSK, one of which he had owned in the past. He now tried to reproduce some of the glories of this roadster in what he called a "contemporary classic".

The Excalibur SS was the result. Stevens had fitted Chevrolet Corvette engines, which, in the 2100lb (952kg) SS, produced a blistering performance of 0–60mph (0–96kph) in five seconds. In style it was evocative of, but not an exact replica of, the SSK Mercedes, and even the brochure was written in pre-war German style! Quality was very high and so were the prices, with the cost of over $10,000 (£7,000) in 1969. Excalibur attracted a celebrity clientele and gained an unstoppable momentum. It still produces neo-classics today, although it is surrounded by other makers who have jumped on the bandwagon.

In Great Britain, a company called Panther did virtually the same thing in the 1970s. The J72 was a pretty convincing replica of another 1930s icon, the SS100. It used modern Jaguar components under a hand-built aluminium body, and the ultimate version had a V12 engine and absolutely phenomenal performance. The cost was twice as much as a Jaguar E-Type and again celebrities, such as the film star Elizabeth Taylor, lined up to buy what was seen as an exclusive convertible.

Perhaps the most opulent neo-classic of all was the De Ville Convertible of 1976–81. This large two-door car was inspired by the Bugatti Royale, right down to its flowing wings and massive free-standing headlights. It had acres of handcrafted chrome on its nose that was dazzled for special effect. Some regarded it as particularly exquisite, while others saw it as being vulgar. For a while it held the questionable honour of being the most expensive car in the world at the price of £30,518 ($45,000). It is small wonder that only six of this exclusive model were ever built.

Below: **The Panther De Ville was a hand-built British neo-classic in the Excalibur vein. In style it recalled the great Bugatti Royale of the 1930s, though it used Jaguar mechanical components. It was this car that was chosen as being the ideal model for the character Cruella de Ville in the Disney film "101 Dalmations".**

CITROËN TRACTION AVANT

Citroën made great play of its Traction Avant, or front-wheel drive, system. During the 1930s, it offered vastly superior road manners and safety compared with conventional cars. Drive was taken from the four-cylinder overhead valve engine to the front wheels via a three-speed all-synchromesh gearbox.

As well as having good road behaviour, the Traction Avant was also one of the world's most beautiful cars. Styled by the gifted Flaminio Bertoni, its graceful curves and low-slung bodyline looked superbly proportioned and exactly right. It presaged many features of cars of the modern era, including a monocoque structure, a luggage

Below: **André Citroën's stroke of genius was to create the Traction Avant ("front-wheel drive") in 1934. In engineering terms it was way ahead of other cars in the 1930s, while in the balance of its proportions it remains as timelessly elegant today as it looked advanced in its own day. It naturally gave itself to the classically French cabriolet style, with two "suicide" doors and a hidden folding roof. Production was confined to the pre-war years.**

Above: **The "Traction" held the road extraordinarily well by the standards of the 1930s, partly due to the front-wheel drive layout and its pioneering monocoque construction.**

CITROËN TRACTION AVANT

⊛ **BODY/CHASSIS** Monocoque chassis with two-door body in steel.

⊛ **ENGINE** Cast-iron in-line four-cylinder overhead valve, 1302cc/1628cc/1911cc, 32–46 bhp.

⊛ **TRANSMISSION** Three-speed manual, front-wheel drive.

⊛ **SUSPENSION** Front: independent by torsion bars. Rear: independent by torsion bars.

27

compartment built into the bodywork (rather than sitting out separately at the back) and wings that were joined to the body, with no gap between them.

Of all the body styles offered, the Cabriolet was undoubtedly the most graceful of all. The two-door body sat on the same longish wheelbase, which added to its elegance. The roof folded completely out of sight and there was a dickey seat (rumble-seat) in the back for extra passengers.

Today the Traction Avant Cabriolet is very sought-after, but it is also quite rare. Unlike the saloon, which continued to be made from the end of World War II until 1957, the two-door Cabriolet was dropped from production in 1940 and was never resurrected. However, if you are searching for a post-war Citroën convertible, look no further than the fabulous Chapron-engineered DS Décapotable, which was offered by Citroën from 1961 to 1971.

Above: **Citroën did not have an official convertible model of its own from 1939 to 1961, after which it offered an extraordinary soft top version of its advanced DS model. The restyling and execution was developed by the celebrated French coachbuilder, Chapron. The so-called Décapotable was the only official two-door DS model and represented the ultimate in sleek lines in its day. Only 1,365 examples were ever built, making this a highly sought-after Citroën in today's classic car market. A number of other independent firms have offered drop-top DS conversions.**

CORD 810

The name Cord was one of the greats of the American car industry in the 1930s. Its front-wheel drive system dictated a long bonnet (hood) that consequently made the cars look particularly fabulous. The early Cords were not very profitable and were withdrawn in 1932, but four years later the nameplate was revived on the superb new 810.

To say that the 810 looked radical is a gross understatement. Its Gordon Buehrig styling was flawless as well as very modern, and notably incorporated concealed headlights (the first in the industry), and wrap-around louvres instead of a grille, as well as exposed exhaust pipes. With its

top down the convertible version looked ultra-clean. The drop-top was available in two body styles, as a two-seater Sportsman and four-seater Phaeton Sedan.

The Cord bristled with many innovations. Having four speeds was a real treat for 1936, while the independent front suspension provided some

Below: **In the 1930s, Cord ranked alongside Auburn and Duesenberg as one of the great American marques. Its 810 qualified as an innovator in terms of both style and engineering. It was a fine-handling machine that was also one of the quickest cars in the world at that time. Two convertible body styles were offered, a two-seater and a Phaeton four-seater, as shown below.**

28

CORD 810

- **BODY/CHASSIS** Separate chassis with two-door body in steel.
- **ENGINE** Cast-iron V8-cylinder side-valve, 4730cc, 125–190 bhp.
- **TRANSMISSION** Four-speed manual, front-wheel drive.
- **SUSPENSION** Front: trailing arms and single leaf spring. Rear: rigid axle with leaf springs.

Right: **No car looked quite so advanced as the Cord in 1936. This was the first car ever to have concealed head-lights, and the horizontal strakes in place of a front grille were a real novelty.**

excellent handling. The V8 engine was supplied by Lycoming, and developed 125 bhp in standard tune. With a Schwitzer-Cummins supercharger bolted on that could leap up to 190 bhp, this was the fastest car of its era, capable of 110mph (177kph) and 0–60mph (0–96kph) in under 13 seconds.

Of course it was not a cheap car at $2145 (£1430) for the two-seater convertible, but it quickly became the first choice of well-heeled types wanting to travel fast in style. However, the Cord was beleaguered by quality problems, and the marque sank in 1937 along with its sister companies, Auburn and Duesenberg. Only a mere 2320 examples had been registered by that time. The Cord is widely recognized as one of the greats of American car design, and there have been many replicas made over the years.

FERRARI 250GT CALIFORNIA

If you were a real car enthusiast in the 1950s and money was no object, the only door to knock on bore the symbol of the prancing horse. Ferrari created superb coachbuilt sports cars in very limited numbers, but with the 250GT of 1954, it almost had an "off-the-shelf" model.

Naturally, there was a convertible version of the V12 powered 250GT, but if you wanted something really special, you could opt for the California. The body looked similar to the "ordinary" Cabriolet, which is not surprising since both were styled by Pininfarina, but it was a little more rakish. The California was specially constructed by Carrozzeria Scaglietti, Ferrari's favoured competition car constructor.

Above: **Chromed air ducts behind the front wheels acted to channel hot air away from the engine bay, as well as looking highly evocative.**

Below: **Of all the many desirable Ferraris, the 250GT California rates in the front row. It has all the right qualities: stunningly beautiful lines, a powerful V12 engine, the right competition breeding and extreme rarity.**

FERRARI 250GT CALIFORNIA

⊛ **BODY/CHASSIS** Separate chassis with two-door body in steel and alloy.

⊛ **ENGINE** V12-cylinder double overhead cam, 2953cc, 240 bhp.

⊛ **TRANSMISSION** Four-speed manual, rear-wheel drive.

⊛ **SUSPENSION** Front: wishbones and coil springs. Rear: rigid axle with trailing arms and leaf springs.

The idea behind the California was that you could take it racing if you wished, and as such it got the tuned 240 bhp V12 engine from the Ferrari Tour de France model. In fact, many owners did take their cars racing, and one even achieved fifth place at Le Mans in 1959. The California had alloy, rather than steel, doors and boot (trunk) lid, saving around 200lbs (90kgs), while the cabin was also more starkly trimmed than was usual for a Ferrari.

After building around 50 cars on a long wheelbase, a new short chassis was introduced in 1960 to save weight and make the car more manoeuvrable. The last California was built in 1962 after a run of only 104 cars. Today, if you are lucky enough to own a California you will be in charge of one of the most prized Ferraris of all.

Above: **The 250GT California was probably the last of its breed: simultaneously one of the best road cars in the world as well as one of the most competitive racing cars.**

Above: **Spin-off hubs were essential for competition, to remove the wheels in the quickest possible time – and this was before the era of pit-lane tyre changes.**

FIAT SPIDER

Although it is often neglected in comparison with the better-known Alfa Romeo Spider, Fiat's own Spider was almost as long-lived, just as popular in its day and very entertaining to drive. It was a real sports car that survived long after just about every other car maker had abandoned sports cars altogether.

Pininfarina created the subtle body styling and, from the car's launch in 1966, it also made the bodies. The mechanical side was derived from the 124 saloon, a car that was a class leader itself in terms of dynamics. The Spider always came with twin-cam engine and disc brakes all round, while you also had the option of a five-speed gearbox. The interior was simple, roomy, civilized and sporty.

The original 1.4 litre engine gradually grew in size to 1.6, 1.8 and ultimately 2 litre sizes. In all cases, performance was a strong suit and all versions were 100mph (160kph) cars, with the fastest model (the supercharged Volumex of the 1980s) reaching 120mph (192kph) and being able to do the standing ¼ mile (0.4km) in 16 seconds.

From 1981, production was taken over completely by Pininfarina and the model was renamed Spidereuropa (or Spider Azzura in the United States). In total, over 150,000 Spiders were made, most of which were exported to the US.

Below: **Just like the Alfa Romeo Spider, Pininfarina styled and built the bodywork for the Fiat 124 Spider. While it may have lacked some of the breeding of the Alfa, Fiat's Spider was certainly not lacking in specification or ability. It went on to become a hugely popular sports car.**

Above: **Italians and Americans took the Spider to their hearts. Its classic good looks, twin-cam engine, smooth transmission and solid handling stood it in good stead. This model is a 1972 California Spider.**

Right: **No one could complain about the Spider's engine, which in all versions was a sweet-revving and powerful twin-cam unit with an aluminium cylinder head. It was offered in 1.4, 1.6, 1.8 and 2 litre versions.**

FIAT SPIDER

⊛ **BODY/CHASSIS** Integral chassis with two-door body in steel.

⊛ **ENGINE** Cast-iron and aluminium four-cylinder double overhead cam, 1438–1995cc, 90–135 bhp.

⊛ **TRANSMISSION** Four or five-speed manual or three-speed automatic, rear-wheel drive.

⊛ **SUSPENSION** Front: wishbones and coil springs. Rear: rigid axle with trailing arms and coil springs.

FORD FAIRLANE SKYLINER

Ford's 1957 Fairlane line-up was one of Detroit's most stylish offerings that year. Unlike the gaudy and contrived excesses of some '57 models, the all-new Fairlane was quite simple and understated, with a clean, full-width grille, bullet tail-lights below restrained tail fins, hooded single headlights and a curved roof-line that was classical in style.

There was one particularly notable model in the Fairlane range, and that was the immortal Skyliner Retractable. Its most

Right: **Straight out of the golden era of jukeboxes, the 1957 Fairlane Skyliner's interior sparkled with chrome and burst with colour. It was a very comfortable environment for up to six passengers.**

Below: **What an amazing party trick! With the roof up the Skyliner looked like a fairly unexceptional two-door hard top, but with the flip of a switch you could witness the roof folding away from over you, neatly doubling up under the rear lid. It resembled an almost impossible and magical cartoon stunt.**

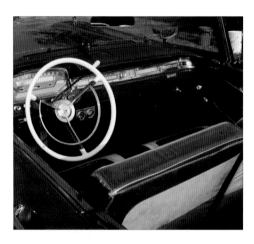

34

Above: **Ford's mid-1950s Fairlane series was fairly prosaic in most respects. The Skyliner remains unique in the grand scheme of automotive history, and its appeal today lies in the novelty of its amazing folding roof. This is a 1958 model.**

Left: **By the time of the 1959 Ford Fairlane 500 Skyliner, demand for the model began to diminish.**

distinguishing feature was a hard top that could fold up and slide under the boot (trunk) lid. The idea may not have been new (the Peugeot 402 also made use of this feature), but history will always regard the Skyliner as the definite item.

The power hard top folded away via a series of dozens of relays and electric motors. It certainly made an impression, but sadly the system was not very reliable and Ford lost $20 million (£13.4 million)

on warranty claims. Demand for the model tapered out during the following two years, and it was axed in the light of a firmer profit-orientated management approach.

Because only 48,394 Skyliners were ever made, they are today regarded as rare classics, that sometimes fetch very high prices among collectors. It remains a monument to an age when Detroit was expanding its horizons with the viewpoint of the sky as the limit.

FORD FAIRLANE SKYLINER

⊛ **BODY/CHASSIS** Separate chassis with two-door body in steel.

⊛ **ENGINE** Cast-iron V8-cylinder overhead valve, 3654–5767cc, 144–300 bhp.

⊛ **TRANSMISSION** Three-speed automatic, rear-wheel drive.

⊛ **SUSPENSION** Front: independent by coil springs. Rear: rigid axle with leaf springs.

35

SPECIALIST CARS

······································

onvertibles are almost always exclusive cars, but right at the top end of the market is a very rare breed of specialist manufacturers catering for the haute couture of automotive tastes. These specialists offer superlative quality, ostentatious luxury and seamless performance.

By reputation alone, at the top of any list of convertibles must sit Rolls-Royce. The Corniche convertible was, in its day, the most expensive open car in the world.

Mechanically, it was based on the Silver Shadow model with its 6.75 litre V8 engine, self-levelling suspension and its automatic transmission. It may not have been the most sporting car around corners but it was the world's most compelling touring car.

The two-door bodywork was initially by the coachbuilder Mulliner Park Ward and was superb in every way, from the harmonious lines to the deep lustre of the paintwork. A Corniche II arrived in 1977,

Above: **Zagato styled the unusual-looking Bristol 412, which featured aluminium bodywork. Pictured is an early 412 with a fixed metal-and-glass roll-over bar and removable targa top and rear sections.**

Left: **Jensen is a British name, but for inspiration the Interceptor looked abroad. As a high-speed grand tourer, it got its engine from America in the form of a giant Chrysler V8, while its handsome bodywork was created in Italy by the coachbuilding firm of Vignale. In combination, the whole of its triple-nationality parts was greater than the sum of its parts.**

boasting a front spoiler and rubber-faced bumpers, and the model lasted right up until 1994, when it was replaced by the Bentley Azure, a convertible version of the stunning Continental R.

Bristol is a tiny British company that is even more exclusive than Rolls-Royce. It produces hand-made cars in very small numbers, but they are almost always coupés. The 412 of 1975–92 was different, since it had a folding roof atop its curiously block-like aluminium bodywork (styled by Zagato). From 1976, the convertible arrangement changed to a novel "convertible saloon" incorporating a fixed roll-over bar and a detachable targa roof and rear panels.

The Bristol was powered by a Chrysler V8 which, from 1982, could be ordered with a turbocharged engine under the name Beaufighter. This could reach 150mph (240kph) and 0–60mph (0–96kph) in under six seconds. Perhaps the best description of this unique motor car is that it is "a gentlemen's club on wheels".

Jensen also used Chrysler V8 engines for its Interceptor. This beast was brutish in character yet it had svelte Italian styling, a beautiful handcrafted body and some generous equipment. It is most often seen in fixed coupé guise. A small number of convertible cars were made between the years 1974 and 1976 (just 267 in all), and they are undoubtedly the most desirable of all. Their power roofs, opulent interiors and very handsome lines mean that these cars are now keenly sought after by many collectors.

Below: **Rolls-Royces are not purchased for their under-statement or modesty. The Corniche represented the most ostentatious model in the Rolls-Royce range, a car that could have been created especially for the Côte d'Azur – indeed its name derives from the mountain range above the coast of Nice and Monaco. There was no more luxurious, nor expensive, way to travel al fresco.**

GYK 598N

FORD MUSTANG

A smash hit is the only way to describe the impact of Ford's Mustang when it arrived in 1964. The original "pony-car" had so much showroom appeal that customers were known to sleep in them to stop anyone else from buying the cars first. Within two years, over one million Mustangs had been sold.

So why, indeed, was the Mustang so very popular? It was Ford boss Lee Iacocca's new idea to create a compact personal coupé as a triumph of style and marketing. As a structure, it was fairly run-of-the-mill, but it had almost infinite combinations of option packages that made it tailored to suit each individual taste: trim, power output, handling packages, power steering, front disc brakes, air conditioning and transmission could all be selected to suit.

The convertible model was one of three body styles, which included a notchback and a fastback coupé. It was a popular choice, but it was never offered with any of Ford's own performance packages such as the Mach 1 and Boss. If you wanted a convertible with speed, Carroll Shelby made GT versions with monster power outputs, and these are today extremely sought-after.

Above: **The original Mustang had great option packs, which effectively allowed you to customize the interior.**

Above: **Classic tail-lights on an early model.**

Right: **Convertible Mustangs made a comeback for the 1983 model year. This is a 1987 Mustang GT Convertible.**

Above: **This was the car that America wanted in 1964 – the Mustang, which invented the idea of the "personal car". Its smart lines, compact size and sporty character were exactly in line with American tastes in the 1960s. Cheap prices and a wide choice of engine and running gear packages added weight to the equation.**

The second-generation 1973 Mustang suffered under the effects of the sad oil crisis and had no convertible option, but the third-generation 'Stang was transformed into a drop-top for the 1983 model year after a ten-year absence. The convertible Mustang was back to stay, a fact proven by the continuation of an open version of the 1993 fourth-generation Mustang.

FORD MUSTANG 1964–73

BODY/CHASSIS Separate chassis with two-door body in steel.

ENGINE Cast-iron in-line six-cylinder or V8 overhead valve, 2788–7030cc, 95-390 bhp.

TRANSMISSION Three or four-speed manual or three-speed automatic, rear-wheel drive.

SUSPENSION Front: wishbones with coil springs. Rear: rigid axle with leaf springs.

Left: **Originally, Mustangs were offered with six-cylinder engines, and in the 1980s a "four" was offered. However, the classic Mustang engine remains the V8.**

FORD THUNDERBIRD

Named after the Native American god of rain and prosperity, Ford's Thunderbird certainly brought the Detroit giant's range of cars a patina of the exotic. It was a direct answer to General Motors' 1953 Chevrolet Corvette, but it set a new tone, not as an out-and-out sports car but as a more luxurious "personal" car.

The 1955 Thunderbird boasted simple, attractive European-influenced lines that were still unmistakeably Ford. It came with a removable glassfibre (fiberglass) hard top. As an option, a soft top was also available. In engineering terms, the T-Bird was quite conventional, deriving most of its parts from the regular Ford line-up, but its ace

Right and above: **Ford had run shy of producing a sports car until the luxurious Thunderbird, which was certainly no ordinary sports car. It was very handsome as well as powerful. The Continental-style spare wheel to the rear was typical of 1950s American styling.**

FORD THUNDERBIRD 1955–57

⚙ **BODY/CHASSIS** Separate ladder chassis with two-door body in steel, hard top, soft top optional.

⚙ **ENGINE** Cast-iron V8-cylinder overhead valve, 4785cc/5113cc, 193 bhp to 340 bhp.

⚙ **TRANSMISSION** Three speed manual with overdrive or three-speed automatic, rear-wheel drive.

⚙ **SUSPENSION** Front: double wishbones, coil springs. Rear: rigid axle with leaf springs.

was a standard V8 engine with up to 198 bhp on tap in standard tune.

The T-Bird was an instant hit, but Ford wanted more volume and so the next generation of cars for 1958 were very different. They were more practical with full seating for four passengers and fussily styled according to the prevailing Detroit fashions and, as a result, they were nicknamed the "squarebird". The theme developed for 1961 with a cigar-shaped profile, and the star of the range was the Sports Roadster with its removable twin head fairings.

By the time the 1967 Thunderbird bowed in, the market had completely changed. Sports car buyers were catered for by the Mustang and the luxury side of the T-Bird was emphasized, leading to the heresy of a four-door saloon version. This generation also marked the end of the road for the soft top Thunderbird.

Top: **The original Thunderbird was a unique car.**

Above left and above: **The third-generation Thunderbird was a dramatically styled GT car of more expansive proportions than before. This rare 1963 Sports Roadster model had sports-style twin head fairings that covered the rear passenger compartment. Its wire wheels and circular tail-lights were very unusual.**

41

JAGUAR E-TYPE

When it first appeared at the 1961 Geneva Motor Show the motoring world swooned at the sight of the Jaguar E-Type. Enthusiasts had become familiar with the gloriously curvaceous D-Type racer in the 1950s, but here was a fully fledged road-going sports car that looked, if anything, even more stunning with its notably rounded body sides.

In more ways than one, the E-Type redefined what a sports car should be. While it was a design masterpiece, its fine XK six-cylinder engine could power it up to a top speed of 150mph (240kph), a speed that was almost unheard of in those days. Even more remarkable was the price, and at just over £2000 ($3000) it was an absolute bargain.

The Roadster was and always has been the essential E-Type, and the fastback coupé, handsome though it was, does not get a look in next to it. As the years progressed, the E-Type got better, with its engine expanding from 3.8 to 4.2 litres, its gearbox gaining synchromesh on all four gears and its brakes becoming larger.

The final incarnation of the E-Type was the 1971–75 Series 3, which had Jaguar's new V12 engine. Once again this catapulted it to the top of the performance tree, and it could do 0–60mph (0–96kph) in 6.4 seconds, which certainly gave the E-Type an extra edge in terms of charisma. As well as this, it had another ace up its sleeve: it had now been given a longer

Right:

Everyone who saw the E-Type for the first time in 1961 could not help but acknowledge its ground-breaking and dynamic shape.

42

Above: **In 1971 Jaguar re-invented the 10-year-old E-Type by installing a brilliant, brand-new V12 engine under the bonnet (hood). This transformed the character of the car, making it the fastest and most comfortable of all the "E" family.**

Above: **The whole nose dramatically hinged forward to reveal the heart of the E-Type, which was its superb XK six-cylinder engine.**

wheelbase, and this meant that, for the first time in an open "E", two children could be seated in the back.

The E-Type left production in 1975 with no real replacement. It is undoubtedly one of the greatest sports cars ever made and, as a result, it has become an icon to a whole generation of enthusiasts.

43

Above: **Curvaceous lines graced the "big cat" E-Type from stem to stern, characterized by the faired-in headlights set behind cowls with indicators above the front bumper.**

Above: **In many ways the E-Type's facia was the epitome of 1960s sports car design, with wood-rim steering wheel, large clear dials and a metal-finished dashboard.**

JAGUAR E-TYPE

⚛ **BODY/CHASSIS** Integral chassis with two-door body in steel.

⚛ **ENGINE** Cast-iron and aluminium in-line six-cylinder or V12 overhead cam, 3781-5340cc, 265-272 bhp.

⚛ **TRANSMISSION** Four-speed manual (optional overdrive) or three-speed automatic, rear-wheel drive.

⚛ **SUSPENSION** Front: wishbones with coil springs. Rear: wishbones with coil springs.

MASERATI GHIBLI

iorgetto Giugiaro was the youthful designer at Ghia who styled the Maserati Ghibli in 1966. Even today, looking back over a career that has spanned many greats, he still regards the Ghibli as one of his best ever designs.

It seems that a lot of enthusiasts agree with him, for the Ghibli, and in particular the Spider convertible, has a fanatical following. In engineering terms the Ghibli followed Maserati's well-known practice. It had a wonderful quad-cam 4.7 litre V8 engine under that long, wide bonnet (hood) that developed a massive 330 bhp. That was enough for a top speed of 165mph (265kph), which was a sensationally fast

Below: **Giorgetto Giugiaro styled the impressively handsome Ghibli, which boasted an ultra-low front end, wide profile and excellent proportions. The Spider version is far rarer and more valuable than the coupé.**

Above: **Pop-up headlights were still an unusual feature in the 1960s, and the Ghibli boasted four lights. By concealing these headlights, the aerodynamics of the nose were improved.**

Left: **Italians really know how to design the interiors of sports cars. The sumptuous cabin featured a flat facia top and an impressive array of rocker switches.**

Left: **Maserati always made its own V8 engines, and the 4.7 litre and 4.9 litre units that were fitted to the Ghibli were among the best powerplant being made at that time.**

45

MASERATI GHIBLI 1966–73

⊛ **BODY/CHASSIS** Integral chassis with two-door body in steel.

⊛ **ENGINE** Aluminium V8-cylinder quad overhead cam, 4719cc/4930cc, 330–335 bhp.

⊛ **TRANSMISSION** Five-speed manual or three-speed automatic, rear-wheel drive.

⊛ **SUSPENSION** Front: wishbones with coil springs. Rear: rigid axle with radius arms and leaf springs.

speed for the time. And in SS tune from 1970 onwards, the engine grew to 4.9 litres and the car was even faster.

The Spider was the convertible version, and it took three years following the launch of the original coupé for it to arrive. When it did, it took people's breath away, for this was certainly one of the most handsome cars on the market. The soft top folded neatly away under a hinged metal cover and a removable hard top was optional.

Of the 1247 Ghiblis made between 1966 and 1973, only 125 were convertibles. They are so desirable that many owners have been tempted to cut the roof off their coupés to make Spider replicas.

MAZDA MX-5 (MIATA)

I f you were a sports car fan in the late 1980s you had but one choice, and this was to buy an Alfa Romeo Spider, a car that was already 20 years old. Every other manufacturer had abandoned sports cars as loss-making and irrelevant.

Then in 1989 Mazda came along and proved them all wrong. The MX-5 (Miata) was not revolutionary or ground-breaking, it was just a great sports car in the traditional sense. Mazda engineers tried to recreate what made the Lotus Elan and MGB great and put it in a modern, reliable, well-honed package. Mazda called it "the return of the affordable sports car".

Above:

In its simplicity and layout, the Mazda MX-5 harked back to the great popular sports cars of the 1960s, such as the Lotus Elan and MGB.

Left: Mazda deliberately fought shy of fitting too many creature comforts in an effort to capture the essence of what makes a great sports car. The cabin design was clear, unfussy and highly effective.

46

MAZDA MX-5 (MIATA)

BODY/CHASSIS Integral chassis with two-door body in steel.

ENGINE Aluminium in-line four-cylinder overhead cam, 1598cc /1840cc, 90–131 bhp.

TRANSMISSION Five-speed manual or four-speed automatic, rear-wheel drive.

SUSPENSION Front: wishbones with coil springs. Rear: wishbones with coil springs.

The MX-5 was simply fantastic. It had a front engine and rear-wheel drive, as well as an open-top, just like the old classics. It was a sheer delight to drive and was plainly far superior in dynamic terms to those great classics.

The cabin was simple, the top was easy to fold away and the equipment was just generous enough. Above all, the little Mazda was great fun with light steering, a gearchange that was slick and fast and exemplary handling.

Drivers took the MX-5 to their hearts, particularly in America. Over the next eight years, over 400,000 cars were produced. The run only came to an end when a brand new MX-5 was launched in 1997. That the original was so absolutely perfect was proven when the new car changed very little of the winning formula.

Above: **No other car of this price bracket offered such a fine blend of exploitable handling, light steering and snappy gearchange. It gave a fun level of performance.**

Above: **Two engine sizes were offered: a base 1.6 litre and the more popular 1.8 litre. Both were overhead cam four-cylinder units made of lightweight aluminium – just the right recipe for high-revving character.**

47

TRIUMPH TR SERIES

Triumph had no real history of sports cars prior to the TR series. It all kicked off in 1952 when Triumph displayed a prototype at the London Motor Show, which was not very well-received. The following year, it was redesigned to become the TR2, and the company's first production TR had arrived.

This was a roadster in the traditional sense. It was rugged, simple and fast. With its 2 litre engine it became the cheapest 100mph (160kph) sports car on the market. Rally drivers loved the TR because it had good ground clearance and was very dependable, and Triumphs began winning numerous trophies. The TR2 grew up into the TR3 in 1955, gaining extra power and refinement.

With the TR4 of 1961 Triumph took a radical new direction: it went to Italy to get a smart new set of clothes from stylist Michelotti. The TR4 was more comfortable and practical and boasted a "Surrey top", or what we would now call a targa top.

Its replacement, the 1967 TR5, was the first British car to get fuel injection and the first TR to have a six-cylinder engine. With more power, performance was far more potent, and this was a strength that was carried over into the TR6, which was the last of the more traditional separate-chassis Triumphs that were particularly popular.

Above: **The first production TR was the TR2, a rugged traditional-style sports car with few frills, a fearsome turn of speed and impressive rallying ability.**

Above: **With its charismatic Italian suit of clothes, the TR4 was very modern. Its Surrey top – a fixed rear window with a removable roof – was a novelty at the time.**

Above: **Fitted with a fuel-injected six-cylinder engine, the TR5 stepped the TR line up into a new performance league, capable of over 120mph (192kph).**

Then in 1975 came the TR7 and everything changed. The controversial Harris Mann styled body looked awkward, only had four cylinders and there was not a convertible until 1979. The V8-powered TR8 helped a little but by then the puff had gone out of the TR line and sports cars in general. The TR factory finally closed in 1981.

Below: **In many ways the TR3 can be regarded as the "classic" TR – a real sports car in every sense, yet with many of the crudities of the earlier TR2 ironed out. Note, for example, the external door handles, which were not a feature of the TR2.**

Above: **The final incarnation of the classic separate-chassis TR series was the TR6, with cleaned up bodywork executed by Karmann of Germany.**

Above: **Despite its controversial shape and compromized specification, the TR7 matured into a respectable sports car, especially in convertible form.**

Above: **The V8-powered TR8 arrived perhaps too late in the day to save the TR family. It was an entertainingly rapid sports car but only 2497 were built.**

MERCEDES-BENZ 300SL

Germany's premier car company is steeped in competition glory, from the great "Silver Arrows" of the pre-war years to current Formula 1 successes. One of the high points was the Le Mans winning car of 1952, which led directly to the creation of the quite magnificent 300SL "Gullwing" coupé.

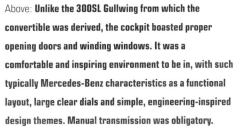

While the Gullwing was a fabulous machine, it had certain drawbacks, notably a lack of winding windows, which was a serious setback in a market where most of the cars were heading towards California. So Mercedes-Benz replaced the Gullwing in 1957 with a Roadster version.

The Roadster was frankly a better sports car. It had a more powerful fuel-injected engine, better rear suspension, proper opening doors and of course a soft top to take advantage of fine weather. It also had powerful disc brakes after 1961.

In other respects the 300SL kept its original virtues, such as alloy opening panels, a floorshift-operated gearbox and a space frame chassis. This was certainly a very fast car, capable of exceeding 150mph (240kph)

Above: **Unlike the 300SL Gullwing from which the convertible was derived, the cockpit boasted proper opening doors and winding windows. It was a comfortable and inspiring environment to be in, with such typically Mercedes-Benz characteristics as a functional layout, large clear dials and simple, engineering-inspired design themes. Manual transmission was obligatory.**

Left: **In character, the 300SL Mercedes was utterly unique. It was an engineering triumph with its racing-inspired fuel-injected six-cylinder overhead cam engine, effective braking and well-located suspension. It may have been something of a handful to pilot but that was simply part of its virtue. In performance terms, it was one of the very fastest cars of its day, being capable of over 150mph (240kph).**

Above: **The 300SL's styling was distinctively Mercedes-Benz. It was one of the most sensational sports cars of the 1950s in terms of performance, echoing the great SLR racers from the beginning of this decade.**

and of doing the 0–60mph (0–96kph) sprint in around 7 seconds.

The 300SL Roadster proved to be much more popular, and today, it is one of the most sought-after Mercedes of all. Ironically the Gullwing is actually worth more, simply because it is a unique design. However the Roadster remains the better car.

MERCEDES-BENZ 300SL

⚛ **BODY/CHASSIS** Spaceframe chassis with two-door body in steel and alloy.

⚛ **ENGINE** Cast-iron and aluminium in-line six-cylinder overhead cam, 2996cc, 225–250 bhp.

⚛ **TRANSMISSION** Four-speed manual, rear-wheel drive.

⚛ **SUSPENSION** Front: wishbones with coil springs. Rear: swing axles with coil springs.

MGB

The name MG will forever have a magic ring to it. It became synonymous with sports car motoring in the years following the war, as GIs returning home to America took their little MG TC roadsters back with them. MG produced the seminal MGA in the 1950s, an exceptionally handsome and capable roadster that managed to combine the starkness of a traditional sports car with modern virtues.

That all changed with the MGB of 1962. Here was an MG with no separate chassis, but with a roomy interior and wind-up windows,

Left: **The great MGA was the direct predecessor to the MGB, and it was a sports car that was perhaps truer to MG's origins in its more Spartan approach. The A had rounded styling and a box-section chassis, the last used on an MG.**

Below: **The MGB could easily be described as the world's favourite sports car. Its popularity stems from its essential "rightness" – sound yet simple engineering, a superb shape and enjoyable dynamics. It is also cheap and easy to run.**

Above: **The tough old 1.8 litre BMC B-series engine remained under the B's bonnet (hood) for its entire 18-year production life. It was extremely reliable, cheap to build and simple to work on.**

Left: **The MGB would do around 106mph (170kph). The interiors were traditional but comfortable.**

53

MGB

 BODY/CHASSIS Integral chassis with two-door body in steel.

ENGINE Cast-iron in-line four-cylinder overhead cam, 1798cc, 62–95 bhp.

TRANSMISSION Four-speed manual or three-speed automatic, rear-wheel drive.

SUSPENSION Front: wishbones with coil springs. Rear: rigid axle with leaf springs.

Right: **Individual details of the MGB's exterior remain well-recognized and well-loved in today's classic car marketplace. The shapely curves of the bonnet (hood) and rounded headlights help to make it one of the most popular and sought-after of sports cars.**

which were previously all heresy at MG. The burly 1.8 litre B-series engine was powerful for its day, while it had an overdrive gearbox and its high final drive meant that the "B" was capable of 106mph (170kph), at the same time posting strong acceleration times.

Successive generations of the "B" watered down the original and handsome conception. Wire wheels gave way to steel, chrome gave way to plastic, the bumpers became Federalized rubber monsters, the sporty ride height increased and power outputs fell. Yet through all that the MGB remained a great sports car.

The MGB is without doubt one of the best-loved sports cars the world has ever known, and it retains its status as one of the longest-lived, finally bowing out in 1980. In roadster form it still remains the archetypal British sports car.

Right: **The famous MG badge, known throughout the world.**

PORSCHE 356 SPEEDSTER

Ferry Porsche started making cars under his own name in 1948 in a small and humble way. By degrees, his company has grown into what has become perhaps the best known sports car manufacturer in the world. One major stepping stone in the growth of the company was the launch of the first Porsche convertible in 1951, and still another was the arrival of the legendary Speedster of 1954.

America had always lapped up Porsches from the start but it soon craved cars with even more performance. The Speedster was conceived for the fast car market, as a light-weight roadster version of the 356. The fact

that it also happened to look so handsome was a feather in its cap at the time, and this is the main reason why it attracts a fanatical following today.

For the new Speedster, some important changes were made; the windscreen (windshield) was cropped by 3¼ inches (8 cm), the padded convertible top was made lighter, and the winding windows were deleted. This saved about 200lbs (508kgs), which certainly helped performance. With the perky engines (1500 and 1500 Super

units, uprated to 1600 in 1956), the Speedster emerged as a very quick little car. In its most powerful guise you could expect a very impressive top speed of 120mph (192kph) and it had a 0–60mph (0–96kph) time of 10 seconds.

While the Speedster was withdrawn in 1958, its legend endured and it is still well respected today. A whole host of replicas have sprung up in recent years, using VW Beetle floorpans as their basis, which was in fact just like the original. Porsche themselves

revived the spirit of the Speedster in 1989 with a very limited run of 911 Speedster models, all of which have features that were modelled on the original design; cut-down screens (windshields), lightweight roof and no electric window winders.

Below: **This view of the standard 356 Cabriolet shows the less steeply raked and taller screen (windshield). This soft top was more sumptuously padded, and there were winding windows rather than side screens. However, it did not make such a lasting impression as the Speedster.**

Left: **With its low roof-line and chopped-down windscreen (windshield), the Speedster not only looked more sporty, but its lighter weight and better aerodynamics ensured that it went much faster. The Speedster model has long since become a legend.**

PORSCHE 356 SPEEDSTER

⊛ **BODY/CHASSIS** Separate chassis with two-door body in steel.

⊛ **ENGINE** Aluminium horizontally opposed four-cylinder overhead valve, 1488cc/1582cc, 55-75bhp.

⊛ **TRANSMISSION** Four-speed manual, rear-wheel drive.

⊛ **SUSPENSION** Front: trailing arms with torsion bars. Rear: swing axles with torsion bars.

SUNBEAM TIGER

In 1962, Texan racing driver and chicken farmer Carroll Shelby shoehorned a Ford V8 engine into an AC chassis to create the immortal Cobra. In 1964 Sunbeam did the same thing with their humble Alpine sports car and created the Tiger.

The result was a true wolf in sheep's clothing. Outwardly the Tiger looked like the Alpine (a roadster based on the floorpan of a Hillman commercial vehicle), and the only way to tell it apart was its full-length chrome body strip and "Powered by Ford 260" badges. But this meek-looking sports car had the teeth to do battle with the AC Cobra. The Ford 260 V8 engine developed 164 bhp and the later 289 unit in the Tiger II had 200bhp. That was enough for a top

Above: **The Tiger lived up to its name in the ferocity of its performance – it could reach 60mph (96kph) from rest in 7.8 seconds.**

Below: **There was little from the outside to distinguish the brutish Tiger from its more effete Alpine sister. One crank of the V8 engine and an onlooker would need no further information to identify this as a Tiger – one of the few British sports cars to challenge the AC Cobra.**

Above: **Twin exhaust tail pipes betrayed the fitment of a Ford 4.3 or 4.7 litre V8 engine up front. Developing up to 200 bhp, the V8 powerplant was an unsubtle but brutally effective means of extracting towering performance.**

SUNBEAM TIGER

- **BODY/CHASSIS** Integral chassis with two-door body in steel.
- **ENGINE** Cast-iron in-line V8-cylinder overhead valve, 4261cc/4737cc, 164–200 bhp.
- **TRANSMISSION** Four-speed manual, rear-wheel drive.
- **SUSPENSION** Front: wishbones with coil springs. Rear: rigid axle with leaf springs.

speed of 125mph (201kph) and a 0–60mph (0–96kph) time of 7.8 seconds.

It was ironic that a Ford engine was chosen when Chrysler had become the major shareholder in Sunbeam's parent company by 1964. Unfortunately, Chrysler's own V8 just didn't fit in the engine bay!

Almost all Tigers were hunted down by American customers, and over the period 1964–68 a mere 7066 examples were made. While they may not have the charisma and ultimate performance of a Cobra (Tigers were substantially heavier), they do have a strong following. After all, there are not many two-seater open-topped sports cars that have a V8 engine rumbling under the bonnet (hood).

TRIUMPH STAG

Four-seater sports convertibles are a genuine rarity. Alfa's GTC and BMW's 2002 Cabriolet both count, but neither can match the sheer charisma of the Triumph Stag. When it was launched in 1970, it was intended to move Triumph into a new market area, the sporting grand tourer that was dominated by the Mercedes-Benz SL, but even this was only a two-seater.

The birth of the Stag was a union of convenient circumstances rather than sound planning. The Italian design house, Michelotti, was solely responsible for the design of the Triumphs during the 1960s and created a styling exercise in 1965 that eventually evolved into the Stag. The attractive final shape was a synthesis of Michelotti and Triumph ideas, featuring a padded T-shaped roll-over bar and generously sized rear seats.

The heart of the Stag was its all-new 145 bhp 3 litre V8 engine. Performance was decent enough at 0–60mph (0–96kph) in 9.3 seconds, and it was very well-behaved around corners, boasting a comfortable ride. But poor reliability harmed its reputation, and production ceased in 1977 after a disappointingly low number of sales: 25,939 all told, of which about a third were exported.

Today, the Stag is highly regarded for its attractive appearance, solid performance and unique four-seater layout. Modern technology and experience can solve all of the original problems, and the Stag now makes a popular choice as an affordable, charismatic grand touring classic.

TRIUMPH STAG

BODY/CHASSIS Integral chassis with two-door body in steel.

ENGINE Cast-iron in-line V8-cylinder twin overhead cam, 2997cc, 145 bhp.

TRANSMISSION Four-speed manual (optional overdrive) or three-speed automatic, rear-wheel drive.

SUSPENSION Front: MacPherson struts with coil springs. Rear: trailing arms with coil springs.

Below: **The Italian design house Michelotti created the Stag's handsome, yet typically Triumph, shape.**

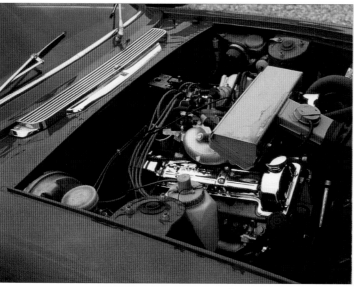

Above: **In action the Triumph Stag was a satisfying animal to drive. Its V8 engine offered quite a solid performance, it certainly cornered with aplomb and boasted a surprisingly good ride for a car of this type. The T-shaped targa roof offered open air motoring to be enjoyed by all four passengers.**

Above right: **The imagery of the Stag somehow suited the strength and purpose of the car perfectly.**

Left: **Rather than fitting the obvious choice of a Rover V8 engine, Triumph slotted in its own, brand new 3 litre V8. While it was a powerful and charismatic unit, its propensity for overheating sadly burdened the Stag with a reputation for unreliability.**

VOLKSWAGEN BEETLE

The origins of the world's most popular car in Hitler's pre-war Germany are famous. It is less well-known that the VW convertible was inspired by an open version of the Beetle built especially for Colonel Radclyffe of the occupying British forces.

In 1949, Volkswagen launched two distinctly different convertibles from two separate coachbuilders. The first was a pretty 2+2 by Hebmüller, but an early factory fire consigned this small company to the history books. The definitive convertible was Karmann's full four-seater with strong sills and door

surrounds to prevent flexing. It really was a well-specified car, with new winding windows front and rear and an elegant stack-up soft top with a proper glass rear window.

While the Beetle rapidly became the world's favourite car, the Cabriolet became a style icon with California cool. It lasted for decades and, while production of the saloon ended in Germany in 1978, the Cabriolet remained in production for a further two years. As one magazine put it, the Beetle became "an institution not an automobile" and today, drop-top Beetles still fetch very high prices in the classic marketplace.

Right: **This is a 1961 example of one of the world's most popular cars.**

The story does not end there, however. VW's Beetle, launched in 1998, is also set to be made in convertible form. Given the frenzy surrounding this saloon (sedan), the convertible version is sure to elicit quite a rapturous response around the globe.

Above: **Volkswagen's 1998 Beetle revives an absolute classic, but the exciting news is that it's set to be made in convertible form as well. The legend lives on.**

VOLKSWAGEN BEETLE

⚙ **BODY/CHASSIS** Separate chassis with two-door body in steel.

⚙ **ENGINE** Aluminium horizontally opposed four-cylinder overhead valve, 1131–1584cc, 25–50 bhp.

⚙ **TRANSMISSION** Four-speed manual or three-speed automatic, rear-wheel drive.

⚙ **SUSPENSION** Front: trailing arms and torsion bars (later MacPherson struts with coil springs). Rear: swing axles with torsion bars.

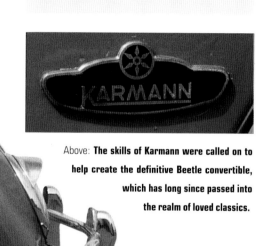

Above: **The skills of Karmann were called on to help create the definitive Beetle convertible, which has long since passed into the realm of loved classics.**

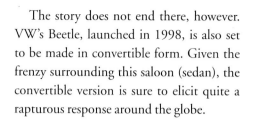

61

FUTURE CLASSICS

MERCEDES-BENZ **SLK**

BMW **Z3**

FERRARI **F355 SPIDER**

Ask anyone who has driven the current crop of convertibles, which one points to the future and they will almost certainly reply, the Mercedes-Benz SLK. The SLK answers all the problems usually associated with soft top motoring: flapping soft tops, leaking and draughty canvas, broken fingernails as you try to raise the roof and so on.

The SLK really is the future of convertible motoring. Ironically, it does not actually have a soft top, instead relying on an ingenious folding hard top. While you are driving with the roof raised, you are effectively in a fixed-head coupé. When the sun comes out, it is a simple matter of pushing a switch and the fun begins. Using myriad electronic relays, the trunk (boot) lid hinges at the rear, the top unclips from the windscreen (windshield) rail, the roof begins to

Above and left: **The Z3 is a model unique in BMW's history – a true sports roadster that is built exclusively at its American plant. Its well-developed rear-drive chassis ensures excellent road manners and its engines – ranging up to a mighty 321 bhp 3.2 litre Motorsport unit – are typically very strong.**

fold over and drop back into the trunk (boot), which swallows it up to leave things completely open and completely clean.

The SLK has other qualities too: superb build quality, a charismatic interior, competent road manners, and a choice of engines ranging from a 136 bhp 2 litre to a supercharged 193 bhp 2.3 litre. And of course it looks like no other car, with its superbly chiselled lines being at once clean and modern, yet inspired by classic Mercedes themes.

Mercedes' main rival, BMW, produces a more traditional convertible sports car that is also guaranteed to become a future classic. Excepting the marginal Z1 of 1988, the Z3 was the first open sports car BMW had made since the 1950s. It gained a real boost when it appeared in the James Bond film *Goldeneye*, and it is unusual in that it is made not in Germany but in a new factory in South Carolina in America. Within 18 months over 40,000 had been sold.

This is a real sports car in every sense, especially in 2.8 litre guise (there were also 1.8 and 1.9 litre versions). Most spectacular of all is the Motorsport powered M Roadster with its M3 3.2 litre 321 bhp engine.

Below: **Ferrari has hardly put a foot out of place with its F355 Spider: performance, engineering, handling and accommodation are all of the very highest order.**

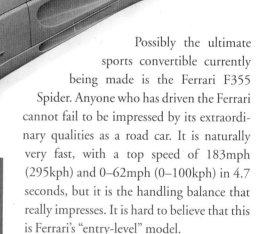

Possibly the ultimate sports convertible currently being made is the Ferrari F355 Spider. Anyone who has driven the Ferrari cannot fail to be impressed by its extraordinary qualities as a road car. It is naturally very fast, with a top speed of 183mph (295kph) and 0–62mph (0–100kph) in 4.7 seconds, but it is the handling balance that really impresses. It is hard to believe that this is Ferrari's "entry-level" model.

Left: **The SLK represents a new departure for Mercedes-Benz, being a compact open sports car. Its most impressive single feature is the quality of design and execution of the folding hard top roof. One touch of an electric switch opens the boot (trunk) up ready to swallow the collapsing roof. Thus the SLK boasts the best of both fixed-head and convertible worlds.**

INDEX

ACKNOWLEDGEMENTS
The publishers thank the following for pictures:
Autocar/The Motoring Archive/Ian Dawson:
p10, 11b, 47t, 61t, 62t, 63. **Classic Cars/Emap**:
p44, 45tr+b. **LAT Photographic**: p1, 2t+b, 3l,
4t+4th from t, 5ltopx4, 6-8, 11t, 12-15, 17t+bl,
20-21, 26, 27tl, 32, 33m, 38bl+tl+tr, 39, 42,
43tr+tl, 45tl, 46, 47br, 48-50, 51b, 52, 53tr+br,
55br, 56-57, 59, 64. Jacket: back flap mr. **The
National Motor Museum, Beaulieu**: p3r, 4b,
16t, 17br, 19, 23t, 24b, 36l, 37, 40, 41t+l, 43b,
51t, 53bl, 62b. Beaulieu/Nicky Wright: p2m, 4
2nd+3rd from top, 5tr, 16b, 18, 22, 24t, 27r,
28-29, 30, 31, 34, 35l, 38br, 41br, 53tl.
Beaulieu/Nick Georgano: p60, 61r. Jacket: all
but back flap mr. **Quadrant Picture Library**:
p9, 23b, 25, 33t, 35tr, 36r, 54, 58.
b=bottom; t=top; l=left; r=right; m=middle.